READ ALL ABOUT IT:

FASHION

ADAM HIBBERT

W

FRANKLIN WATTS
LONDON

This edition 2004

Franklin Watts
96 Leonard Street
LONDON EC2A 4XD

Franklin Watts Australia
45-51 Huntley Street
Alexandria NSW 2015

Copyright © Franklin Watts 2000

First published in 2000 and 2004

Series editor: Rachel Cooke
Assistant editor: Kate Newport
Designer: John Christopher, White Design
Picture research: Sue Mennell

A CIP catalogue record for this book is available from
the British Library.

ISBN 0 7496 5677 8

Dewey Classification 302.4

Printed in Malaysia

Acknowledgements
Cartoons: Andy Hammond pp 6, 9, 15, 20; Sholto Walker p 14–15.

Photographs: Front cover: Rex Features: main, crb; Popperfoto:
tr (Reuters/Gareth Watkins); Oxford Scientific Films: cra (Mike Hill); Back cover: Rex Features. Insides: Camera Press pp. 4t (Patrick Litchfield), 11b (Trevor Leighton), 21tr (Stewart Mark); Corbis pp. 16t (Gail Mooney), 23t (AFP); The ELLE website, designed in conjunction with Hachette Filippachi (owners of the ELLE brand) Actif Group plc (owners of the ELLE clothing license for Europe) and Zoom p. 27;Format Photographers pp. 12c (Jacky Chapman); Image Bank p. 26b (Guido A. Rossi); International Fund for Animal Welfare p. 13t (© The Wild Yak Patrol); NSPCC p. 23b (© Dominic O'Neill/Nguyen); Panos Pictures pp. 8 (Heldur Netocny), 9 (Roderick Johnson); Popperfoto pp. 3b (Scanpix/Erik Johansen), 4b (Reuters), 5 (Reuters/Gareth Watkins), 11t (Reuter/Jean Christophe Kahn), 13b (Reuters), 20, 21b (Reuters/Dylan Martinez), 25 (Reuters/John Schults), 26t (Duncan Willets), 29; Rex Features pp. 3tc, 10, 14b, 16b (Steve Wood), 18 (t & b), 19b (Steve Wood), 21tl (Sipa Press), 24; Topham Picturepoint pp. 3tl, 6 (Peter Jordan), 7t (Ben Curtis), 7b, 12t (Owen Humphreys), 17 (Neil Munns), 22 (Fiona Hanson); John Walmsley p. 12b; Franklin Watts p. 28; Wellcome Trust Medical Photographic Library p. 19t.

EDITOR'S NOTE

Read All About It: Fashion takes the form of a newspaper called *The Fashion News*. In it you can find a lot of articles about a lot of different subjects and many facts. It also includes opinions about these facts, sometimes obviously as in the editorial pages, but sometimes more subtly in a straight news article: for example in the article concerning the use of fur in fashion (page 13). Like any newspaper, you must ask yourself when you read the book 'What does the writer think?' and 'What does the writer want me to think?', as well as 'What do I think?'.

However, there are several ways in which *The Fashion News* is not and cannot be a newspaper. It deals with one issue rather than many and it has not been published on a particular day at a particular moment in history, with another version to be published tomorrow. While *The Fashion News* aims to look at the major issues concerning fashion and body image today, the events reported have not necessarily taken place in the past few days but rather over the past few years. They have been included because they raise questions that are relevant to the issue today and that will continue to be so in the future.

Another important difference is that *The Fashion News* has been written by one person, not many, in collaboration with an editor. He has used different 'voices' and, in some instances, such as the letters and opinion pieces, pseudonyms (they are easy to spot!). However, the people and events reported and commented on are real.

There are plenty of other things in *The Fashion News* that are different from a true newspaper. Perhaps a useful exercise would be to look at the book alongside a real newspaper and think about, not only where we have got the approach right, but where we have got it wrong! In the meantime, enjoy reading *The Fashion News*.

THE FASHION NEWS

Home News 7

Skinny Posh – a bad example?

Careers 18

It's not just clothes that give you style

Sport 28

Parents pay for the latest club strip

FASHION VICTIMS?

The News Editor

Latest figures suggest that as many as 1% of 15-35-year-old British women suffer from the eating disorder anorexia nervosa – that amounts to an astonishing 75,000 cases.

Some experts are alarmed by the statistics, while others are relieved, noting that no significant growth in cases has been recorded in the ten years since the last survey.

ANOREXIC

Anorexics suffer drastic weight loss, premature ageing and fragile bones. The bingeing asssociated with the disease is also very damaging to health. In the worst cases, anorexia leads to death.

The report will add to the controversy over the use of extremely thin models in fashion. According to campaigners, low self-esteem and negative body image among young women are caused by comparing their figures with those of the top models. Most women cannot slim down to these sizes without seriously damaging their health.

In response, fashion editors point out that the market that they need to appeal to most is 16-30-year-old women. Within that age bracket, a slim physique is not uncommon. ■

NO BUSINESS LIKE SNOW BUSINESS

The fashion world flocked to Disneyworld, Paris, this week. But don't worry – you won't all have to wear red shorts, white gloves and big Mickey ears next season. The world's fashion buyers were there to snap up the latest styles in snowboard and skateboard chic. Over 700 small and medium-sized designers were at the GlissExpo, dressed to impress – further evidence that fashion is no longer about elitist chic, but expressing yourself and your lifestyle. ■

The casual styles of the snowboarder are flying high in fashion.

GOVERNMENT SAYS FATTEN UP! See page 7

INSIDE NEWS: Home news 4–7, Foreign news 8–9, Health and Beauty 10–11, Education 12, Environment 13, Editorial and Letters 14–15, Business and Careers 16–19, People 20, The Fashion Culture 21–25, Travel 26, IT 27, Sport 28–29, Directory 30–32

The Unkindest Cut

The News Editor

Elizabeth Emanuel, the designer who created the late Princess Diana's wedding dress, may be forced to sell off-cuts and calico mock-ups of the dress to pay money to her creditors, according to *The Sunday Times*.

Lawyers acting for her creditors, owed a reported £300,000 by the designer, are keen to put the leftovers up for auction in New York. Ms Emanuel placed them in a trunk after completing the dress for £1,050 in 1981, but had no intention of releasing them for sale.

'Everyone is drooling over it – it makes me sick,' the paper reports Ms Emanuel to have said. The designer wants the materials kept in Britain, possibly at the Victoria and Albert Museum in London, where they could go on public display.

TO DI FOR!

Diana memorabilia has risen significantly in price since the Princess died in 1997. But even while the Princess was still alive, her association with leading fashion names made her a style icon. Seventy-nine dresses that auctioned in the year of her death raised £3.4m for charity (£43,000 per dress). The princess's fans who bought the dresses now find that the dresses may be worth up to double the price they paid. ■

The late Princess Diana in her wedding dress.

Everyone's Dahling!

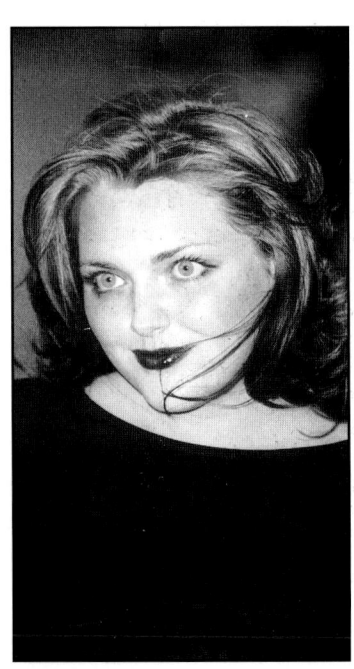

Fashion magazine *Marie Claire* recently confronted its readers with the option of 'larger' model Sophie Dahl (left) or 'sex-kitten' Pamela Anderson on its front cover. Circulation figures clearly demonstrated that Dahl was the readers' choice- but Dahl was not impressed! The model turned author has since dropped from a reported size 16 to a size 10 by adopting a strict diet and exercise regime. ■

HAUTE STREET FASHIONS

British fashion will never be the same again. For the fourth year running, cutting-edge styles from Britain's most influential young fashion gurus will be available on everyone's high street.

Hussein Chalayan, renowned for his show-stopping stunts at London Fashion Week, and three other major talents, are signed with Arcadia, the retailing mega-corporation behind Top Shop, Dorothy Perkins, Principles, Evans and Racing Green.

In return for the hours spent tweaking their catwalk designs to suit the mass-production methods a high-street retailer requires, the designers receive double benefits. Their taste and style is instantly available to a much larger market; and the big pay packet they receive enables them really to splash out on their top-end artistic work. Without high street cash, the fashion shows just wouldn't happen.

In return, Top Shop has benefited by association. With the Top Shop logo appearing in many a catwalk photo, customers understand that the brand represents a hotline to the heart of style. ■

MALE ORDER

More men are shopping for clothes than ever before

The big news at the retail end of the fashion industry is that brothers are doing it for themselves. Men have traditionally had their clothes bought for them by mothers, girlfriends, wives and assorted female friends. Apart from a small youth market in fashion-conscious urban 20-somethings, men have treated shopping with approximately the same level of enthusiasm as going to see their dentist.

Demographic changes have finally laid this old stereotype to rest. With women earning as much as – or more than – their male partners, men are taking on some of the roles traditionally associated with houseproud wives. From making the weekly shopping trip to the supermarket, it's a short step to browsing through clothes shops and taking more responsibility for personal appearance.

Designer labels are making the most from this trend. Men are more likely to seek status than low prices when they buy their own clothes. Partly as a result of their novice status in the market, men are more likely to pick up on highly recognisable brand names as a guide to quality. ■

SUITS YOU, SIR!

The statistics reflect the change in male shopping habits. In 1978, a survey of shopping patterns by *Progressive Grocer*, a New York-based trade publication, found that about 10 per cent of the main shoppers in each US household were men. In 1998, the magazine found that this statistic had risen to 17 per cent.

American figures also show rapid growth in menswear sales. The all-American male spent $35 billion on clothing between January and September 1998, up from $32.5 billion during the same period in 1997. In other words, menswear is growing faster than any other market segment. ■

Watch out, girls! The boys are hitting the high streets – and they mean business...

Just don't do it?

Nike's first ever report of a decline in profits was met with joy in certain quarters. *The Daily Telegraph* newspaper hoped this might indicate that young people were abandoning street style for a more elegant look, but carried this ironic warning: 'While parents must feel overjoyed to see their children looking attractive and walking normally, they should keep quiet. Parental approval of clothes is the kiss of death.' ■

No-shock shocker!

The News Editor

Is British fashion finally **growing up? London Fashion Week boasted** its usual crop of topless or near-enough naked models in the less established collections, but there was a definite sense that such tabloid stunts have had their day.

In the past, London's new talents had to leave a nipple exposed here and there to guarantee themselves any press coverage. In Milan, Tokyo, Paris and New York, the media's attention is focused more on the quality of the clothes themselves than on the models' bodies.

But now the Brits seem to be settling down to some serious work. Established and new designers alike were more interested in beautiful clothes, built for real women. In contrast to previous years – where, for just one example, Chalayan sent a model down the runway wearing nothing but an Islamic veil over her face – all the big names concentrated on wearable collections. Perhaps now our best talents won't feel they have to set up in Paris to be taken seriously. ■

Seriously chic? London Fashion Week plays it straight.

SKATE BETTYS HIT TOWN

There can't be many cities in the Western world that lack a concrete corner where teenagers congregate to display their skateboarding skills. Skaters now form a huge leisure sector in their own right, worldwide, and their slacker styles often dictate what happens in the high street this time next year.

So if non-clothing trends in the skate world are anything to go by, look out for a sudden plague of Skate Bettys in a town near you. A Skate Betty is a girl, typically between the ages of 12 and 16, with baggy trousers and tiny lurid crop top, short hair and spangly pins, who hangs around skate corners admiring the talent.

A Skate Betty is not a skater. Indeed, her biggest joy, apart from swooning over some accomplished amateur stunt-boy, is to snigger with glee when a would-be Girl Skater takes a public tumble.

Otherwise, her day is occupied in talking with her girl gang and juggling the group's mobile phones as hot gossip flies from one end of town to the other.

If you're tempted to jump on the Betty bandwagon, try buying a skater's magazine from an independent music shop or newsagent, and check out the adverts. The brand names to die for change by the hour, so be prepared for some fancy footwork — and some potentially heavy spending. And all that's before you even set foot on a skateboard! ■

MODEL AGENCY EXPOSED

A television document-ary exposing drug abuse and sexual misconduct at a top model agency has shocked the modelling world. It has also cast further doubts on the ethics of using young girls as models. The agency, Elite, was the subject of a year-long undercover investigation by the BBC series, MacIntyre Undercover.

Using hidden cameras and microphones, the document-ary followed contestants as young as fifteen as they competed to become Elite's new Talent of the Year. The

programme revealed an agency employee supplying illegal drugs to a young model, and an agency executive boasting about his sexual exploits with previous contestants.

APOLOGIES

John Casablancas, Elite's Chairman, issued a state-ment from the agency's Milan office offering 'uncon-ditional apologies' for the 'shocking, unacceptable and totally incorrect' behaviour of some of the agency's employees. A specific apology

A MODELLING CAREER? TURN TO PAGE 19

Are young girls, like these 14-year-old competition winners, safe on the catwalk?

was made to the families of the young contestants, for Elite's failure to ensure that their girls were properly looked after while in Elite's care. Certain staff members

have been suspended while the agency awaits the results of an internal inquiry.

Former Elite models include Cindy Crawford and Naomi Campbell. ■

FATTEN UP

The government is urging the fashion industry to change its attitude to women's bodies. A working group of leading members of the fashion world, including several magazine editors, met Minister for Women Tessa Jowell in Downing Street in June, 2000. Ms Jowell reported that she had won promises to

Posh Spice on the catwalk – her weight provoked more comment than the clothes she was wearing.

reduce the use of skinny models, blamed by some psychologists and health campaigners for promoting unhealthy dieting and anorexia among young women and some men.

New research in Germany

SKINNY STARS

has underlined the dangers of the eating disorder, anorexia, often linked by campaigners with fashion's obsession with the slimmest of models. Dr Stephan Zipfel, of the University of Heidelberg, found that 10% of reported cases are still suffering after 20 years, and a further 16% have died as a

result of the disorder.

But there is controversy over the statistics – whilst some awareness groups claim that as many as 3.5 million people suffer from eating disorders in Britain, others put the figure at less than 100,000.

In addition to anorexia, fad dieting is on the increase. Although most teenagers do not have eating disorders, research suggests that up to half of 13-14 year olds limit their eating to stay slim.

There is also concern at the other end of the scale – while anorexia cases have remained static recently, obesity is rising dramatically. ■

No Logo

Foreign Affairs Editor

When Canadian journalist Naomi Klein published her book *No Logo* in January 2000, she hit a nerve .

No Logo was a bitter and persuasive account of the 'crimes' that companies commit by reducing global culture to designer labels.

Klein's idea was that there is a new kind of business, centred around selling people lifestyles, labelled with a brand.

Critics argued that companies have been doing this for decades, and that other forces were more important in the movement of industries to cheaper countries, such as the high cost of manufacture in Europe and the US.

However, Klein's insight into world of international fashion brands and their sweatshop factories did not seem to affect the buying public much, despite the popularity of her book.

What was needed was an organisation who could guide fashion producers onto a more 'ethical' business model. The task of making ethical clothing is a complex one. For example, closing a sweatshop factory may save poor people from bad work, but other ways for them to earn money must be found first.

Enter the Fairtrade Foundation, already established as a 'logo' which can only be added to ethical products. Fairtrade have a good record of support for ethical producers of simple goods such as coffee.

FAIRTRADE

In 2003, Fairtrade's Harrriet Lamb announced that the organisation was planning to establish labelling for the market, starting with simple fabric items such as bedsheets and underpants: 'We're not looking to license some highly complicated full outfit of clothing. We'll start with simple products such as bed linen and underclothes, then move into the more fashionable end of the industry.' ■

The right to go to school

One thousand children marched against sweatshops and domestic work in Delhi recently, demanding their right to go to school. Up to 32 million Indian children are kept out of school by work. ■

Working children

The Save the Children Fund estimates that 61% of working children live in Asia. Working children on average account for a quarter of a poor family's income. But only 5% are in paid work for export, such as clothing manufacture. Most work as an extra pair of hands for their parents, for example on small farms. ■

Stop Sweatshops campaign

The Stop Sweatshops campaign in Canada has launched a Clean Clothes campaign, with an activists' pack, complete with profiles of companies, such as Nike and Woolworths, who have been criticised for using cheap labour. There are also tips for further research. ■

Two young girls in a factory in Bangladesh making clothes for export to the West.

Don't Fake It!

Designer Hilfiger wins $6.4m compensation for fakes sold by Wal-Mart

'Designer' watches? Some fakes aren't so easy to spot.

Wal-Mart Stores Inc. has employed a specialist in counterfeit clothes to vet all its suppliers, after losing a five-year court battle with Tommy Hilfiger, the designer clothing label. Wal-Mart was found to have been selling fake Hilfiger products as the real thing. Remaining Wal-Mart stock of fake Hilfiger clothing has been donated to charity.

Hilfiger boss Joel Horowitz hoped that the ruling would alert customers to the fact that even reputable high street chains can sometimes get it wrong.

'Many people don't realise that counterfeiting exists not just at the level of the street vendor, but also in large retail chains,' he said.

US Customs officials seize huge quantities of counterfeit goods each year. 'US companies lose millions of dollars in potential sales when an imposter hijacks their brand name and passes off frequently inferior merchandise as the real deal,' said a Customs Agent, Awilda Villafane. 'In 1997, Customs officers around the country seized $54 million worth of counterfeit goods.' ■

CAIRO COUTURE

Wealthy Egyptians packed Cairo Opera House to welcome the city's first major international fashion show. Top designers from Europe and elsewhere, including Christian Lacroix, Emanuel Ungaro and Pierre Balmain, brought their latest collections to Cairo's high society before moving on to the oil-rich Gulf States of the Middle East.

SAFELY STYLISH

Spaghetti-strap dresses and short skirts were as risqué as any of the designers would go, however. Even very wealthy Middle Eastern women dress conservatively compared to Europeans and Americans. But what they miss in exposure, they more than make up for with a sharp eye for good taste. ■

NOW THAT'S A LOUD SHIRT!

Howies, the American skate-style pioneer of street fashions, has caused controversy with a new line of T-Shirts, called 'Shoplifter'. The shirts boast a large barcode that is designed to trigger the theft alarms in many high street stores. David Hieatt, Howies' spokesman, explained the brand's use of such stunts: 'When you don't have the money to compete with the big boys you have to out-think them'. Howies' gimmick is just the latest of a range of new advertising strategies explored by smaller designer labels to get around the boredom and cynicism of a media-savvy youth market, confirming the brand's 'underground' or 'subversive' status. ■

IT'S NOT THAT YOU NICKED IT, YOU'VE PASSED YOUR 'USE BY' DATE....

Skinny models off the hook?

An unusually thin woman perhaps, but not an unusually thin model.

Over the last five years, ultra-thin catwalk models have been blamed for widespread eating disorders among teenage girls. Counsellors working with the worst cases of anorexia and bulimia, in particular, argue that images of very thin women cause low self-esteem among teenagers of average weight.

But a report just published casts doubt on the connection. A team of psychologists at the University of Texas says that their study contradicts previous research. One group of girls was given a subscription to *Seventeen* magazine, while another read no fashion magazines. 'Body dissatisfaction' was measured at the end of the study, and showed no significant difference between the groups.

Dr Eric Stice, leading the research, is confident that his study of 219 teenage girls has produced the most accurate picture of the problem to date. 'I think the media reflects a larger cultural pressure for an ultra-slender body,' Doctor Stice concluded. 'Parents, peers and dating partners may play a more important role than the mass media.'

Gilly Green, a psychotherapist at the Centre for Eating Disorders in London, remained unconvinced, saying that the findings were based on too small a sample over too short a period. Media images, particularly on TV, have been strongly implicated in an alleged 'outbreak' of eating disorders on the Pacific island of Fiji, which only adopted television in 1995. According to Harvard University's Anne Becker, an anthropologist who has studied Fijian diet and standards of beauty since 1988, 'Nobody was dieting in Fiji 10 years ago'. Now 74% of teenagers report that they feel 'too fat'.

However, as a study of eating disorders by the Institute of Psychiatry at the University of London concludes, on the information available no one can say for sure whether or not the eating-disorder problem is growing. ∎

VITAL STATISTICS

- On any given day, there are 48m Americans dieting.
- A third of Australian women diet.
- In the United Kingdom, there may be up to 3.5 million people suffering from anorexia and bulimia.
- 16 percent of American women have made themselves vomit in an attempt to lose weight.
- Fashion models weigh 23% less than they did 25 years ago. ∎

BREAST AWARENESS

Stella McCartney, the designer and daughter of Linda and Paul McCartney, has lent her support to the campaign to raise women's awareness of breast cancer.

Ms McCartney made the move after her mother died, aged 56, as a result of the disease. 'It's a really tragic thing when you have experienced breast cancer. The death of a loved one when it is seemingly unnecessary is very, very painful,' she told Sky television.

'The only positive thing you can really gain through losing someone is learning, and teaching other people. So I hope to teach other people and I hope to learn,' she explained.

According to some estimates, as many as one in 11 British women will develop the disease at some point in their lives. Early detection of lumps in the breast can dramatically improve the chances of recovery.

Stella McCartney also uses her high profile in the fashion industry to support the animal rights cause, something dear to her mother's heart. ■

Stella McCartney in her workroom.

Breaking the size barrier

We have all had that awful frustration of finding an article of clothing we love – but the shop just doesn't have it in the right size. For some – the very tall, the very small, the very broad and even the very skinny – this experience is the rule rather than the exception.

Clothes can only be made cheaply enough for the high street if manufacturers can run off hundreds and thousands of identical garments. But some people have an unusual body shape that excludes them from this market. On top of the teasing and insults they often have to face in public, it can be terribly de-moralising for men and women to find that the clothes they need aren't available. In this way, high-street fashions only underline society's narrow definition of what is 'normal' and 'beautiful'.

There have long been specialist shops for those people whose bodies aren't accommodated by average-sized clothing, but finding out about them has been difficult. Now, it seems help is at hand through the Internet (see panel). Perhaps fashion for all will now become a reality. ■

Designer Helen Teague and comedienne Dawn French have done much to promote fashion for larger women.

SITES OF INTEREST

These are just a few of the websites springing up to cater for all kinds of body-shape.

■ www.highandmighty.co.uk
the site for the men's retailers for tall or rotund men.

■ www.longtallsally.com
New on the web, but long-established as retailers for tall women, Long Tall Sally brings simple design, and a practical, friendly approach.

■ www.petitestyle.com
A webzine for shorter women with information on useful retailers.

■ www.extrahip.com
A spirited (but not so practical) site for bigger women, celebrating plus-sizes and promoting the retailers who cater for them.

■ www.sixteen47.com
Designer fashion for larger women. Sixteen 47 was set up by comedienne Dawn French and designer Helen Teague. Not selling on line yet but good for a browse. ■

Skirting the Issue

Pupils at Wickham School, Gateshead, face a new uniform choice after a landmark case. Schoolgirl Jo Hale, 14, has won the right to wear trousers to school, with the support of the Equal Opportunities Commission.

It took her three years, but the school finally backed down as Jo prepared to take her case to a European tribunal. But despite her victory, the decision won't affect school rules elsewhere in Britain. Jo's mother, Claire Hale, backed her daughter completely. 'I hope the outcome is influential in other cases where silly rules discriminate against girls,' she said. The case was settled 'out of court', meaning that the legal arguments have yet to be tested before a judge.

Nevertheless, from September 2000, the uniform at Wickham School must permit girls as well as boys to wear the school-approved dark grey trousers. No boy has yet tested the new equal opportunities policy by wearing a skirt, but after David Beckham's sarong, it can only be a matter of time… ∎

No trousers, please...

Trousers as we know them were first worn in the early 1800s, though they caused alarm at the time. Priests in Sheffield were forbidden to wear them, and the Duke of York was turned away from his gentleman's club in 1814 when he arrived in a pair. ∎

Jo Hale with her mother Claire. Her mother has backed Jo in her fight to wear trousers at school.

Should Schools Say No to Fashion?

The Education Editor

People have been mugged in Los Angeles for the sole purpose of making off with their 'latest thing' trainers, but do school children here face the same fate?

The main problem facing parents world-wide is the expense of keeping children in clothes which won't make them a laughing stock in the playground. Many see school uniforms as the solution. They prevent the nasty competition that can develop over fashion essentials, such as designer footwear, and also save parents money. In Britain, uniforms cost an average £14 less than the equivalent 'everyday' clothes. However, few children would opt for uniform given the choice. ∎

VITAL STATISTICS

A survey for retailer Woolworths of 1,000 parents with kids at primary schools in the UK found that:

- ■ 2% kit their offspring out with a cap
- ■ 3% buy blazers
- ■ 27% of boys wear a school tie
- ■ 83% of primary school children wear a uniform
- ■ 91% of parents approve of school uniforms ∎

Fur's Fair?

Fake fur may promote real fur

There was a muttering in the aisles at the Millennium's catwalk shows in Paris, as it emerged that fur was definitely back in designers' repertoires.

Some love it, some loathe it, but for the past ten years fur clothing has been the sole preserve of Russian mafia molls, not famed for their good taste. In the West, wearing a mink or sable coat has become a social no-no equivalent to eating children, and the fashion conscious follow super-model Naomi Campbell in declaring 'I'd rather go naked than wear fur!'

Developments in fake fur technology may be partly to blame for the return to fur. The ubiquitous 'fleece' top of the late nineties resulted in real sheepskin popping up in the most stylish wardrobes. Now with visionary designers such as Yohji Yamamoto trimming

their hats and shawls in luxurious fake furs, the return of natural furs seems certain.

Yamamoto has escaped the ire of anti-fur campaigners. His fake fur collection on show in Paris was apparently considered to be politically-correct. No-one seemed to mind that many of the Japanese design guru's outfits were constructed from suede. And barely an eyebrow was raised when Naomi Campbell took a spin on another runway in a stunning pair of mink high-heels.

FUR CRAZY

Naomi's not the only one to rethink fur, though. So many collections used it in 2003/04 that a girl model would have been jobless if she had stayed fur-free. ∎

"We'd rather go naked than wear fur."

Every fur coat means animals died a painful death by electrocution, drowning, or being gassed. DON'T WEAR FUR!
For more information please write: PETA P.O. Box 42516 Washington, DC 20015 USA

PeTA
PEOPLE FOR THE ETHICAL
TREATMENT OF ANIMALS

Top models get naked to promote an anti-fur campaign.

Chiru fawns, orphaned by poachers, are fed by hand.

Blood-stained Wraps

The end of the 20th century saw a sudden hunger for exotic shawls and wraps sweep the fashion world. But as the passion for the Pashmina shawl dies off, so too have populations of the rare antelope whose fur is used to make its replacement, shahtoosh wraps.

The endangered Tibetan antelopes, called Chirus, live only at 14,000 feet on the Tibetan steppe. International trade in Chirus was banned in 1975, allowing the population to recover to about one million animals, but poaching in recent years has reduced that number to a mere 75,000 survivors.

Poachers use machine guns

to bag several Chirus at once. At least three of the tiny animals are required to make a single shahtoosh wrap. But the fine-wool wraps fetch up to £10,000 each in the West. Shahtoosh means 'king of wools' in Persian.

INNOCENT BUYERS

New York has cracked down on fashionable people who have innocently bought one of the wraps – most believe that the wool is gathered by hand. But as Dr George Shaller of the Wildlife Conservation Society says, 'Every person who wears a shahtoosh has the bloody bodies of at least three Tibetan antelopes on his or her shoulders'. ∎

Editorial

STOP THE ROT!

The fashion world has never made great claims for its own social importance. At best, fashion provides us with a space for self-expression and play. If the industry is criticised for frivolity and irrelevance, so much the better. When it comes to the crunch, we can always point at the alternative – the blue pyjama-suits made compulsory in China under Chairman Mao – and suggest to our critic that he take his pick. But the complacency that this suggests won't do. We cannot dismiss fashion as simply fun, when so many serious issues surround it.

The catwalk in particular is a source of disquiet, as more campaigners argue that there is a link between ever-skinnier models and a rising tide of eating disorders among our young. Catwalk models themselves are more likely than ever to be considered slaves to a vicious machine that demands inhuman sacrifices.

But the problems don't stop there. Commerce has long been a dirty word in arts circles, but this attitude is becoming more mainstream. Fashion is nothing if not the cutting edge of commerce – it's there to make money! Young people are under pressure to beg, borrow or steal the latest 'in' thing, and fashion drives them ever onward. The fashion industry is an easy target for criticism for anyone who is suspicious of money-makers and international corporations.

To stand up to this criticism, fashion requires a clearer voice. The occasional charitable venture is fine, but no better than any number of boring businesses manage. Fashion really needs a champion, an outfit that can respond to the snipers in a calm and sympathetic manner. Because if the industry fails to broadcast a positive image, no one else will.

Fashion trades on that rare human emotion, joy. There are a lot of killjoys out there who would like nothing better than to stifle and control this trade. Who's to stop them? ■

Letters

The Trousers Issue

Sir –

I can hardly believe my ears. I learn that Cheltenham College for Young Ladies, long recognised as one of the last principled arbiters of taste and elegance in this country, has allowed the young ladies to wear trousers. Must every nook and cranny of society be purged of the charms of femininity?

Unreconstructedly,

Booey Tradescant

Big is Beautiful

Sir –

What a delight it was to see Sophie Dahl on the catwalk after the years of super waifs and heroin chic. I thought the fashion world had turned its back on twig-like models.

Even so, isn't it scandalous that, five years later Sophie the only full figured catwalk

'name' we can think of has now succombed to pressure and lost three dress sizes.

Hungrily,

Lydia D'Orly Quarante

Does it matter?

Sir –

I was horrified to read yet

another article which condemned the Duchess of York for her choice of outfit. Maybe it wasn't the latest in chic and perhaps it didn't show off her now-slimmed-down figure to perfection, but does it matter? Surely more important was the fact that she was speaking at a meeting to promote AIDS awareness – something your reporter seems to have conveniently forgotten.

Yours unfashionably,
Supporta Royal

Sophie Dahl, the only well-known full-figured model.

Something to talk about:
SHOULD CHILDREN FOLLOW FASHION?

No!
Wally Woolley

Yes!
Ivor Style

Dear Ivor,

I suppose I must begin by saying that I'm no enemy of fashion. I know that it brings joy and colour to our humdrum lives, and would be sorely missed if we tried to do without it.

However, children do not need the extra burden that being trendy places on them. Fashion is for adults to express themselves with. Nothing is more horrible than expecting a child to impersonate an adult.

Yours, Wally

Dear Wally,

I'm glad we've established that you don't have objections to fashion, as such. Let's concentrate on why you might object to fashion in children's lives.

I happen to think that children are fashion's most important fans. Children are immensely sensitive to the way they fit in, and love to experiment, in ways that are far beyond boring old adults' abilities.

Yours, Ivor

Dear Ivor,

It's exactly because of children's sensitivity to peer pressure (fitting-in, as you phrase it) that fashion is best kept out of the playground.

If one has poor parents, or parents who are less keen on frivolous clothing than one's friends' parents, terrible teasing and social isolation can result.

Yours, Wally

Dear Wally,

Children have to learn how to negotiate life's pitfalls for themselves. One of the hardest things to learn is how to influence the way people relate to you. Experimenting with fashion is part of this learning process. By changing how they look, kids learn how unimportant appearances truly are!

Yours, Ivor

Dear Ivor,

If it were that simple, I would have no problem with your argument. Sadly, some children, for a variety of reasons, are denied an equal chance to 'experiment'.

I would rather see children in uniforms. As any teacher will tell you, children will always find a way to express themselves through minor 'improvements' to a dress code. And none of them need feel excluded.

Yours, Wally

Dear Wally,

I remember my brothers insisting that Mum 'take in' their trouser legs in the 80s, when the school trousers were too flared.

Uniforms will always be customised, more often than not by put-upon mothers. Why is that any better than other clothes?

As for the expense, keep up! Most modern fashions are more influenced by the charity shop than £100 gymshoes.

Yours, Ivor

Dear Ivor,

It seems that you don't mind if our children believe that they can buy affection by spending money on their appearance.

I believe that children should learn to value each other and themselves on the basis of their personalities, not on the cut of their trouser legs. Wouldn't the world be a nicer place if our kids could rise above shallow consumerism?

Yours, Wally

Dear Wally,

You have finally confessed that you are uneasy with fashion, after all. For you, fashion is all about money and shallow consumerism.

It doesn't have to be that way. Fashion is about expressing your personality. Only those silly enough to worship cash in the first place choose fashions that are exclusive because of the designer price-tags.

Yours, Ivor

Woman of the Week

Finance Editor

When Ming sees a new product that really hits the spot, you know about it – with a wink and a clap of the hands, she sparkles enthusiasm, and makes lightning-quick decisions. According to Jeffrey Pfeifle, a senior product design executive, the knack is her personal touch – 'She's definitely a toucher and feeler'.

Ming heads up Gap's next-generation of clothing stores, Old Navy, where she has worked as a top executive since Gap launched the brand in 1994. With the experience of a woman devoted to fashion buying all her life, Ming's decisions about which products to adopt could make or break the Old Navy chain – the shop has to pre-buy huge stocks to make sure that they don't run out when they hit upon the season's must-have clothing item.

So far, her instincts have done the retailer no harm at all. With 450 shops across America, and an expansion planned at around 2 new branches each week, the Gap subsidiary looks set to overtake Gap stores themselves as the company's core money-earner, bringing in just under $4 billion in 1999. ■

An Old Navy store, the next-generation to Gap.

GUCCI TAKES ON YVES

The famous YSL logo will be an excellent addition to Gucci's empire.

Luxury goods company Gucci has snapped up the Yves Saint-Laurent brand for an estimated £625 million, with a pay-off to its two founders of approximately £40 million.

Gucci has recently staged a huge comeback under the direction of Domenico de Dole and creative direction by Tom Ford. The Italian style has been given a new, trendy twist, increasing sales by over 400%. Now, with an equally well established label alongside it, profits look likely to soar.

The YSL business 'fits' well with Gucci's expertise in accessories. According to an industry analyst at Credit Suisse First Boston, 'Now that Gucci controls the YSL trademark, they can enhance the brand by introducing new products, like shoes and bags – it will be a whole new revenue stream for Gucci.'

NEW FRONTIERS

The acquisition is the first purchase the Gucci group has made outside Italy, and is sure to upset The era of the great supermodels may be in decline, but a new trend is emerging in the modelling scene - start out as a model, become a movie megastar!

Dressing down

Many major city-based firms are abandoning the old-tradition of the suit and tie in favour of 'dressing down'. Leading banks, such as Lehman Brothers, found they were facing a recruitment problem, with many graduates opting for companies with less 'stuffy' dress codes. However, not everyone is happy with the change. Whereas a suit is a safe and easy buy, 'smart casual' means putting more thought and time into what you wear – and reveals to all your individual sense of style. ■

THE END OF THE SUPERMODEL?

MODELS TURNED ACTRESS MAY BECOME EVEN MORE COMMON?

Supermodels like Naomi Campbell are looking after their futures.

Since the heydey of supermodels such as Naomi Campbell and Kate Moss, having a celebrity face has become increasingly important for all kinds of jobs beyond the fashion industry.

In recent years cosmetic companies have chosen celebrities such as Andie McDowell, Catherine Zeta Jones, Elizabeth Hurley, and Beyonce rather than just models to front their major campaigns.

ARTISTES?

The change was dramatically illustrated in November 2003 when it emerged that two agencies were battling over who 'owned' a clutch of modelling beauties. Elizabeth Jagger, Erin O'Connor, Vivien Solari, Alek Wek and Jade Parfitt all had contracts with Model 1, a fairly traditional modelling agency.

They 'defected' to ICM, a global theatrical agency with major links with the movie business. ICM may well represent the future of modelling - think, for example, of what it has done for the post-modelling career of one of its 'hot properties' - Cameron Diaz. ■

Fame costs!

Uberbabe Kirsty Hume recently discovered how harsh fame and fortune can be. The newspapers are always looking for juicy gossip, and Kirsty's two uncles have delivered. They told the press that the model ignores her granny, even failing to invite her to her wedding with popster Donovan Leitch. Whatever Kirsty may think, the message for aspiring models is clear: if you don't want your private life made public, don't be famous! ■

Sweet Smell of Success

Thinking about a career in the fashion industry? It's not just to do with clothes. *The Fashion News* went behind the scenes to meet the people who work to make us smell beautiful.

The director

As director of one of L'Oreal's main perfume units, Cacharel, Dimitri Katsachnias had to bring a new perfume to the market that young, aspirational women will buy every bit as readily as a Chanel No5 refill.

Perfume, known in the trade as 'the juice', sells to an extremely volatile market. There are around 3,000 established ingredients from which 'the juice' may safely be built, and the packaging and advertising messages are, if anything, even more complicated.

The 'nose'

Katsachnias began by assembling a fresh creative team and briefing them to conjure up a product that captured the mood of the women he expected his perfume to appeal to – pure, strong, calm and determined. Perfumier

Olivier Cresp, a professional 'nose', set about building the new juice from around 15 unusual ingredients, including peony petals, blackcurrant and coffee.

The designer

As Cresp worked on the vital contents, packaging designer Annegret Beier set to work translating the brief into both the glass bottle, and the box it would be wrapped in. Each element of both items must be easy to produce in huge quantities without loss of quality.

The marketing expert

At the same time, marketing expert Tho Van Tran began the tricky business of designing an advertising campaign that would catch women's attention, appeal to them, and intrigue them enough to look out for the bottle on their next department store visit. Television advertising is extremely expensive, and it's down to Van Tran to ensure that the right message gets across before the money runs out.

The financier

Of course, as with any big business, there are accountants and people with money to invest who want to understand whether the new product is likely to do well or not. Since Cacharel are sure to be enthusiastic, there have to be other people they can turn to for expert advice. Big merchant banks and stockbroking firms employ people to understand each trade. So Susanne Seibel, perfume industry analyst at Merrill Lynch, can tell us all about the new juice's prospects.

The prospects

Of around 150 major launches each year, extremely few become hits, and fewer still manage to retain a loyal following for decades. But as Susanne Seibel points out: 'You start with a ladies' perfume. Then you come up with shower gels, body lotions, soaps, a men's fragrance. Then a follow-up for the ladies. You expand the life cycle.'

CLASSIC STATUS

Nobody knows if Cacharel's new juice can achieve the success and familiarity that eventually bring a new perfume up to classic status. But if it does prove to be a hit, the rewards can be enormous. Chanel's No5 perfume has raked in profits of up to 20% for several decades now, and shows no sign of flagging. How has it achieved this success? In the end, nobody really knows ... ■

SO YOU WANT TO BE A MODEL?

If you're thinking of modelling, you'll soon find that there are a lot of people and organisations out there who look as though they can offer you some help. But only a few of them are really taking your potential seriously. The rest are there to cash in on your eagerness.

Models who have made it suggest that you visit four or five of the best model agencies you can travel to easily. A little research in advance can save you being tricked into 'signing' with an agency that has nothing going for it. Don't get over-excited if one of them offers to put you on their books – unless two or three can see your potential, you're better off reconsidering your career at this stage.

The trouble is, you may be really tempted by an agency's offer, and then you have to decide whether to invest your hopes (and your money) in taking it up. ■

A model poses patiently.

Warning signs to look out for include:

High-pressure sales techniques. If you're told that there's just one opening, if you can sign immediately, you're almost certainly being taken for a ride.

In-house photographer, or 'one-stop' portfolio compulsory. They may well be about to charge you over the odds for some amateur snaps. Always ask to see the photographer's portfolio, and look for several 'tear sheets' from well-known fashion magazines, clearly credited to the photographer. Portfolios must be built up over time – a one-stop portfolio tells potential clients that you're an amateur.

Vague guarantees of work. Nobody can promise that a client will take a shine to your look. The best indicators are to enquire about other models' careers handled by the organisation.

Remember: conmen always do best when the person to be conned really wants something badly – they know how to turn your dreams to their advantage. Be wary! ■

Young model Sarah Thomas's career has really taken off.

Obituary: Gertrude Shilling 1910–1999

Gertrude celebrates her media profile in style!

Born Gertrude Ethel T. Silberston at St John's Wood, London, on March 3rd 1910, Gertrude Shilling was known and loved throughout the fashion and racing worlds for her extravagant hats.

Her father's trade was making bearskins for the Guards, and her milliner son, David Shilling, made his first Ascot hat in 1966, aged 12. Perhaps inspired by Cecil Beaton's black and white costumes for the film, *My Fair Lady*, the hat was a metre across, with stunning black and white frills.

Fashionable society was amazed when Gertrude made her appearance at the races, and photographs of her were rushed to London to make the evening news. From then on, her regular appearances at Ascot became an institution, almost as important as the horses.

Her hats became ever more daring, in 1977 leading the Clerk of the Course to turn her away from the Royal Enclosure when her red, white and blue 'jubilee' hat proved too large to pass through the entrance.

She married Ronald Shilling in 1940. After the war, Ronald set up a successful clothes manufacturing business, with a speciality in fine shirts. He died in 1988.

Gertrude Shilling was given 18 months to live in 1966 after being diagnosed with breast cancer. After part of one breast was removed in the late sixties, she became the first person in Britain to undergo a breast implant.

Gertrude will be remembered for her willpower in battling cancer, her extraordinary sense of fun, her charity work, and, without question, for transforming the way we think about hats. ■

PEOPLE WATCHING

Mouna Ayoub

Having made her fortune as the wife of an enormously wealthy Saudi Arabian, Mona Ayoub returned to Europe, with a divorce and an estimated £61m in the coffers. She has since been credited with single-handedly rescuing haute couture from economic ruin. Estimates of her clothing budget hover around £15,000 per week – enough, certainly, for her to have amassed over 150 Chanel outfits. Understandably, not all of them can be accommodated in even the most lavish walk-though wardrobe, so La Ayoub flogs her seconds off at charitable benefits.

Wacko Paco?

Has Paco Rabanne become too eccentric for the Parisian fashion scene? The Spanish-born elder statesman of high fashion, who has lead the pack in Paris for over 30 years, seems to be tiring of the luvvie life. After slamming Chloë head designer Stella McCartney's work as 'grotesque and pitiful' in a magazine interview, Mr Rabanne raised eyebrows when he moved his 1999 exhibition date to avoid being in the French capital city on August 11th – he was allegedly convinced that Paris would be crushed by the Russian space station Mir falling from the sky. ■

Is Fashion the New Art?

 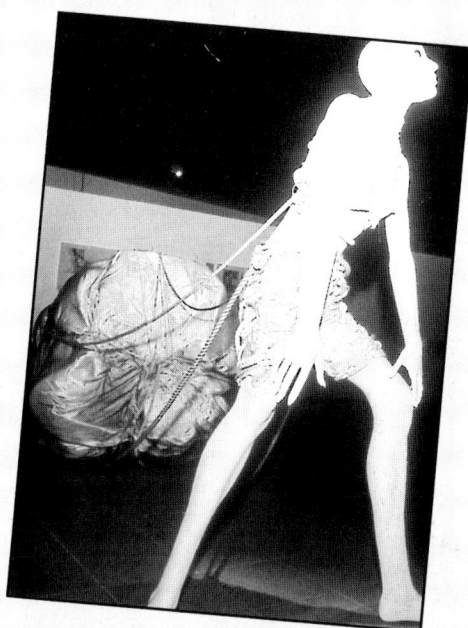

The 'Mondrian' dress (left); Christo's wedding dress (right).

Since as far back as the 1920s, the worlds of high fashion and high art have been closely associated. Max Ernst, a founder of the Dada art movement, famously pronounced: 'Let there be fashion. May art die!' The Dada-ists encouraged art lovers to treat art with less respect. Ernst included an axe with one of his sculptures, inviting gallery-goers to smash it up.

At the same time as art was being knocked from its pedestal, fashion was to be treated more seriously. Fashion pioneers such as Elsa Schiaparelli led the way. In Paris in the late 1920s and 30s, she brought surrealist art to the clothing world with a dress printed with the image of a desk, with 'drawers' for pockets.

Schiaparelli worked with art world conspirators such as Salvador Dali, Jean Cocteau and the photographer Man Ray. The fashion industry gradually realised that its designs need not only be about clothing. They could just as well function as works of art. Yves Saint-Laurent's famous 'Mondrian' dress was certainly wearable, but appeared to be cut from a canvas by the famous modernist painter.

Other designs were created as works of art, and were never intended for use. Christo is a contemporary artist famed for wrapping large buildings and whole islands in fabrics. His wedding dress is an elaborate joke on the heavy responsibilities of marriage. Made in 1967, the 'dress' is bound by heavy ropes to a 20-ton pile of silk-wrapped boulders. This 'train' would have utterly immobilised any bride who made the mistake of trying to wear it.

Paco Rabanne's first collection was called '12 Unwearable Dresses'. Like other clothes designers from the 1960s onwards, he delighted in high-tech fabrics, exploring their potential far beyond the limits imposed by the needs of everyday use. The new Japanese trend-setters, such as Issey Miyake and Yohji Yamamoto, also found no clear distinction between art and fashion. Their clothes range from ready-to-wear to impossible sculpture.

For all this cross-over, though, it seems that the two worlds are still separate. If you can use an item as practical clothing, its usefulness makes it hard to think about as an art object. If an item is utterly unusable, however, it instantly stands out as an artistic statement. In the end, fashion is devoted to finding pleasant ways to cover our bodies. Art, it seems, still refuses to get its hands dirty with such everyday concerns. ∎

Alexander McQueen's design is hardly practical, but is it art?

Fashion Police

HRH Queen Elizabeth II dressed in 'Stonehenge' style?

There's one Top Ten listing that no celebrity wants to appear in – that of Hollywood's bitchiest fashion critic, Mr Blackwell. Every year, the self-made Sheriff of Style County publishes a list of the world's worst-dressed women, to the amusement of all but the poor celebs he has singled out.

The critic doesn't simply pin-up his Most Unwanted posters, though, but goes on to provide simple soundbites to add insult to injury. In previous years he advised Kate Winslett to leave her wardrobe aboard the Titanic, described Mariah Carey as 'shrink-wrapped cheesecake', and even dubbed the Queen with a new honorific, 'Stonehenge of Style'.

Mr Blackwell claims not to enjoy the task which has earned him his international fame. Last year he complained: 'It is not a pretty sight. It's a year that has seen an endless stream of couture catastrophes and fashion blasphemies.'

Betting on this year's front-runners is hotting up. If you're a female celebrity in the vicinity of Los Angeles, be very careful to avoid the fate of actress Sandra Bullock. What do Hollywood success and big pay cheques count for, when you are sure to be remembered by Mr Blackwell's description of you as 'a Victorian lamp-shade on the loose'? ■

Lonely work

A model's life can seem to be the ultimate in glamour to ambitious young men and women, but for the superstars the glamour can soon wear thin. Being in demand around the world means long months away from home, living out of a suitcase and in the company of strangers.

Even if a Naomi Campbell or Elle Macpherson only has to spend an hour on a catwalk or a photo-shoot, the schedule is punishing. Particularly during the seasonal shows, models are rushed from one location to another. Unlike any other hard-travelling people, they have to arrive looking as if they have just stepped off a cloud, not red-eyed and jet-lagged.

Coping with the pressure, without the support of friends and family, can be too much for some. International models have to be content with their own company, but not to the point of dreading the moment when the hairdresser knocks at five in the morning.

So next time you hear of a super-model throwing a tantrum at some airport, pause before you titter. Travel is a tiring business, and most of us have stamped our foot in a train station at some time. Why should models be any different? ■

SHOULD FASHION MIX WITH POLITICS?

No one thinks twice when a fashion celebrity lends their support to a 'good cause'. Cancer research and the NSPCC are just two of many that the fashion world has taken up and used all its promotional skills to support. But what about more overtly political causes: can the frivolity of fashion mix with such controversial matters as animal or even human rights?

Back in 1996, the Co-Operative Bank had a scuffle with fashion bible, *Vogue*, over an advert it planned to run in the glossy style magazine. The advert showed laboratory animals undergoing tests, inviting anyone sickened by the pictures to join the bank and boycott animal testing. *Vogue* refused to run the advert, and the Co-op accused the rag of censoring them to keep rich cosmetics companies happy. *Vogue*'s publishing director Stephen Quinn rejected charges of censorship, explaining that his readers would find the adverts 'tediously controversial'.

In 2000 Benetton, whose 'United Colors' advertising has always courted controversy, provoked a particularly violent reaction against their latest campaign. This features images of men on death row in the US, including Jerome Mallet, sentenced to death for killing a police officer in 1985. Benetton stores have been picketed and Benetton face a million-dollar law-suit. Benetton claim that the campaign is genuine and that advertising, so much a part of our mainstream culture, is as legitimate a way to promote discussion of the rights and wrongs of the death penalty as a newspaper column.

The trouble, as with many

Jerome Mallet as featured in the Benetton campaign.

issues related to fashion, is money. Benetton cannot simply claim they are raising awareness of the issues, they are also promoting their name – and selling jumpers. Perhaps *Vogue*'s apathy is more frightening, but could it be more honest? ■

T-SHIRTS FOR CHILDREN'S CHARITY

Actress and model Liz Hurley has been thrilling the paparazzi again in a revealing Versace outfit – this time for charity. The British celebrity, along with other top models, was promoting a special Versace-designed T-shirt in aid of the NSPCC's Full Stop campaign.

The campaign, which is also supported by the Spice Girls and Madonna, aims to end child cruelty with a

Three models show off the 'Full Stop' T-shirt.

number of public awareness initiatives.

DARING OUTFITS

Hurley has been linked with the Versace label ever since she wore a daring Versace outfit detailed with safety-pins to the premiere of *Four Weddings and a Funeral* five years ago. Since then her dresses have been show-stoppers at a number of film premieres.

Donatella Versace, now head of the family's fashion empire, said that she felt a strong sense of duty to use her high profile, and her customers' fame, to draw people's attention to the less visible members of our society, especially children.

The T-Shirt costs £15 and is available through mail order from *Hello!* magazine, as part of its pledge to raise £1m for the Full Stop campaign. The campaign, supported by the Duke of York, began in 1999 and attracted mass celebrity backing. ■

FLOGGING A DEAD CLOTHES HORSE?

What are the catwalk shows for, if not to inspire and amaze the clothes-buying public? The exposed nipples and outrageous accessories that characterise modern collections are clearly not created for Mrs Bloggs on her Saturday nights out.

Catwalk shows, for the last quarter of a century, have been all about dazzling the media. Make the fashion glitterati rave about the bravery or vision of some impossible outfit, and the brand name of your fashion house earns priceless advertising. You actually don't need to sell those ridiculous rags. What you do sell are plain old cosmetics, accessories and luggage, with the edge of glamour only your designer label can provide.

But what's this? The overwhelming media response to the Paris catwalks at the turn of the millennium was a weary cynicism. An entire platform at one of the city's main train stations covered in sand for a Saharan performance? Yawn! Naomi Campbell as Pocahontas, strapped to the front of a train? Dahling, is that the time, already?

Believe it or not, the fashion of the moment is to be bored with such grand gestures. The fashion editors are claiming to be confused by the irrelevance of it all.

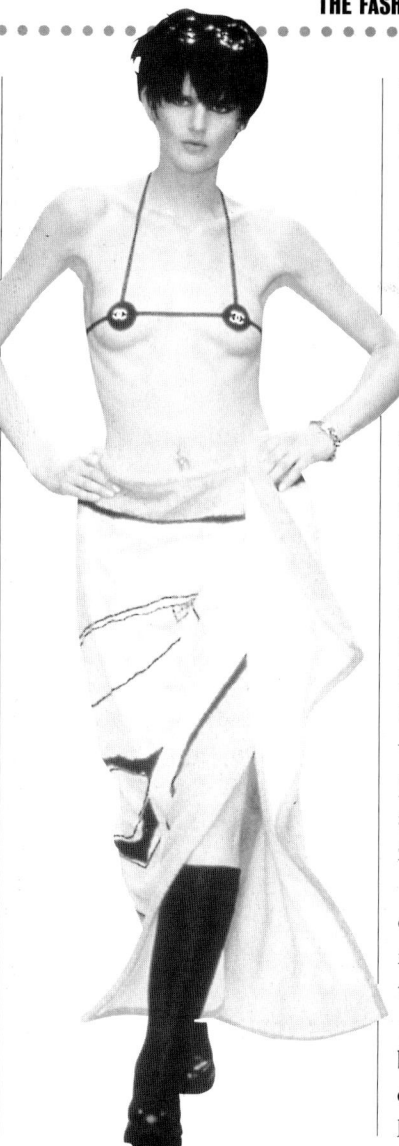

Where are the cocktail dresses, the everyday suits, the casual wear?

As ever, Jean-Paul Gaultier proved himself ahead of the pack. The designer, who made his name pulling off spectacular stunts with outrageous bad taste, came up with a collection that had the weary hacks purring with delight. The clothes were wearable, the styles bulging with street cred. Karl Lagerfeld's collection for Chanel also hit the spot. No elaborate Elizabethan costumes here – Lagerfeld's new Chanel suits were all simplicity, to the point of frayed edges and simple, concealed fastenings.

Could it be that haute couture is returning to reality with a bump? Or is this cry for simplicity just a pause to gather strength before the next round of extremism? In fashion, as in life, only time will tell. ■

From the hip

■ 'Fashion doesn't cause bad feelings about your body. It certainly doesn't cause anorexia or eating disorders – any more than Country and Western music causes alcoholism and adultery.' **Valerie Steele, Curator, Fashion Institute of Technology Museum, New York**

■ 'Now it is the power of the nipple! The nipple is always outside, it's terrible. You see it on every catwalk. You see the nipple. You see the bottom. It is nice maybe for men, but it is not something a normal woman should wear.' **Sophia Loren, actress**

■ 'Fashion can be regarded as the story of the fictitious body as a visible surface' **Akiko Fukai, Chief Curator, The Kyoto Costume Institute**

■ 'Brevity is the soul of lingerie.' **Dorothy Parker, writer and wit**

■ 'Although [modern women's] nudity appears the same as that of primitive people, it is quite opposite in reality, as their bodies are covered with invisible and infinite fashion.' **Takaaki Yoshimoto, Japanese cultural guru and father of Banana Yoshimoto**

■ 'There are no ugly women, only lazy ones.' **Helena Rubenstein, cosmetics house**

■ 'With a black pullover and ten rows of pearls, she revolutionised fashion.' **Christian Dior, on Coco Chanel**

■ 'The corset was worn not only to suppress vitality, but also to gain in cachet.' **Thorstein Veblen, social scientist**

■ 'Never fit the dress to the body, but train the body to fit the dress.' **Elsa Schiaparelli, early 20th-century fashion pioneer**

■ 'Art produces ugly things which frequently become more beautiful with time. Fashion, on the other hand, produces beautiful things which always become more ugly with time.' **Jean Cocteau, French surrealist** ■

A FASHIONABLE LIFE: JEAN-PAUL GAULTIER

Jean-Paul Gaultier in sensational mode – and enjoying it!

The designer who made Madonna's outfits world-famous was born in a Parisian suburb, Arcueil, in 1953. His first ideas for clothes were for his mother and grandmother, when he was eight years old. At 17, he submitted a handful of sketches to Pierre Cardin and was taken on board as an assistant. From that point forward he has consistently delighted and outraged the fashion world with his outlandish creations.

DEMOLITION!

One Givenchy designer is reported to have summed him up thus – 'His style isn't design, it's demolition. It is sensational for sensationalism alone, provocation for provocation's sake. It is bad taste in all directions.'

It is for just those qualities that Gaultier has conquered the heights of the fashion industry. Ironically, now that he's there, his designs have calmed down and he seems to be becoming more user-friendly than all the other designers in Paris put together. ■

A cosmetic change?

What's good enough for Alexander McQueen, top Parisian designer, is also good enough for growing numbers of ordinary men. McQueen famously had liposuction recently to lose weight, shedding 6.5kg at a stroke.

New research shows that the market amongst men for plastic surgery has more than doubled over the last five years. In America, sales of men's hair dyes have risen from $18 million to $100 million over the same period.

In Britain, the new, image-conscious man is causing a minor boom for cosmetics companies. Julie Howard of Clinique reports that the company's sales to men increased by 25% in 1999.

Men may have been buying women's skin-care products 'on the quiet' for a number of years, but repackaging the same ointments with macho names has helped men overcome their reluctance to be seen taking care of their appearance. Almost all men, that is – Clinique expects its new website to lead to even more sales, since men will then order their products over the internet for mail-order delivery, with no risk of running into their drinking buddies at the cosmetics counter. ■

BE SCENE!

If you're planning a break in spring, why not take a month out and 'do' fashion's most fabled destinations? Join the fashion pack as they globe-trot from one metropolis to another, sighing and giggling over the latest collections from talents great and small, and – most importantly for the cities themselves, spending lots of money. Our handy guide to the season starts here!

Early February

NEW YORK

The Big Apple is not the warmest place on Earth in February. Pack plenty of thermals, and remember the importance of layers! These are the places to see and be seen:

Nuyorican Poets Café, 236 East 3rd Street

In the heart of fashionable Chelsea, the Nuyorican (it's a play on the local accent, if you're wondering) invites its patrons to roll up their sleeves and pitch in with a few verses of your own. You don't have to be Shakespeare to enjoy yourself, but it helps.

Mary Boone Gallery, 417 West Broadway

Any Europeans in town for a week with cash to burn can find plenty of irreverent artworks for sale here. Postmodernists of the 80s and 90s are a house speciality.

Mid/late February

LONDON

There is so much young talent on the London circuit that you'll drop dead of exhaustion if you try to make every show. Work out which ones everyone else is going to, and ignore them. You'll be reading their reports tomorrow, so why not go somewhere truly obscure and earn yourself some Brownie points? Otherwise, you could drop in at:

Harvey Nichols, Knightsbridge

The fifth-floor restaurant is fabled for illicit encounters and ladies who never stop lunching. Grab a window seat and amuse yourself guessing who your fellow diners might be.

Matsuri, 15 Bury Street

Keen on the Japanese food fad, but oh-so bored of all that zen minimalism? Go subterranean at this expensive eaterie and have a performing chef juggle amazing meals over a hot plate, right before your eyes.

Late February/ early March

PARIS

The capital of chic, Paris oozes style from every pore. The high point of the fashion calendar, the Paris shows are the most talked about, the most stunning and most influential of the year. Sell your grandmother to get a seat in the front rows. Otherwise, try out these hot spots:

Café Charbon, 109 rue Oberkampf

Simply too trendy to describe. Don't bother showing up with last year's accessories.

Café Marly, Musée du Louvre, Rue de Rivoli

Beneath a wing of the world-famous art museum, home to the Mona Lisa, you can take a tipple on the terrace and enjoy the spectacle of the uncompromising glass pyramid architecture.

Web Bar, 32 rue de la Picardie

Only in Paris would an internet café attempt to relieve the boredom with salsa nights, concerts, exhibitions of art, cinema and live storytelling. Excellent for checking out the news from the catwalk shows you missed. ■

Will eTail kill Retail?

ELLE
Women's Wear
Women's Accessories
ELLE Passion
Children's Wear
ELLE Trends

ELLE Shop Info
Conditions of Sales
Change Your Password
View Your Basket
European Stores

ELLE Online Shops

ELLE shop
Spring Summer Collection 00

ELLE is also "prêt-à-porter", fashion accessories, interior design items ... all of which are exclusively created for ELLE or carefully hand-picked by our ELLE PASSION experts.

Europe

A present !

Search

Shopping made easy? Or less fun? Welcome to e-tail.

Clothes shops may prove to be the last businesses left in city centres after the internet revolution, according to a study of electronic commerce, or 'e-tail'. Consumers are avoiding difficult trips around major shopping areas in favour of ordering goods over the internet and having them delivered to their front door.

But shopping for the latest fashions is one of the few activities that the Internet seems incapable of replacing with a more enjoyable alternative. Customers need to feel fabrics and test how outfits suit their colouring and shape. And there's no substitute for the simple business of trying clothes on in a dressing room.

Until now, that is. A US retailer has teamed up with programmers Broderbrund, to produce a virtual shop on a CD-Rom. For around £30, American women with a basic desktop computer can create a virtual model, based on their own measurements, which they can then use to try on a catalogue of clothes.

A VIRTUAL MODEL

Cosmopolitan Fashion Makeover, the program, allows the home consumer to view the results from any angle, and even to add their own scanned-in face to the 3D model. So even clothes shops may not be safe from the information revolution.

But if the computer still doesn't appeal, Parisian couture shops are pioneering a happy medium. Shop assistants with a webcam on their shoulder are now ready to assist you in finding that vital garment. ■

FASHION WEB

You may not have to travel the world to see the latest fashions, just log on. Here's our guide to who's www.hip and who's a www.blip

HIP

www.dressforsuccess.nl
A directory similar to Yahoo or Google, but dedicated to fashion, organised into themes such as 'window shopping' and 'history of fashion'.

www.fashionwindows.com
Everything a fashion retailer needs to know, from the best new designers and styles to suppliers of fashion dummies.

**Toronto Fashion Incubator
www.fashionincubator.on.ca**
A great site for would-be fashion designers with an amount of experience and a need for business support.

**First View
www.firstview.com**
You can catch up with the latest collections, almost as they appear (for a price), or scan back over your favourite designer's previous works – for free!

**Elle
www.elle.com**
Elle has a more exclusive look and feel than *Cosmopolitan*, catering to the kind of women who care what's being discussed around posh dinner tables in the world's capital cities. There are also useful art and museum guides in there for the jet-set culture vulture. ■

BLIP

**GQ (Gentleman's Quarterly)
www.gq-magazine.co.uk**
This is just a marker page for Britain's most established style magazine for men, driven by an appreciation of the female form. There is very little content to look at, which only serves to make the paper version seem more likely to bore the average web user. Unimpressive.

**Fashion 18
www.fashion18.com**
This Canadian teen fashion site works hard to please, but it looks like a breakfast cereal carton.

**Fluxuries
www.fluxuries.com**
An example of the thin line between being so fashionable it hurts, and just being a pain.

**Supermodel
www.supermodel.com**
If there's anyone out there who hasn't been bored to death with the minutiae of these famous models' lives, be our guest. After five minutes of this tedious site, you'll find it a thrill to watch paint dry. ■

Clubs Stripped of Money Spinner?

The football task force is listening to parents' complaints about the cost of football strips

A young boy proudly displays his England strip.

The football task force headed by conservative MP David Mellor has submitted its proposals to the government. The task force looked at all aspects of the sport that might be helped by official guidelines.

TEAM COLOURS

Recommendations include forcing clubs to keep the same strips for a minimum of two years, and requiring the shirts to have a fixed 'sell by' date printed in the collar for supporters' information. The measures are suggested to prevent clubs using changes of outfit to squeeze money from fans, and parents in particular, who want to wear their team's colours.

The report suggests that the government set up a regulatory body to deal with footie fans' concerns. The body would negotiate a Code of Conduct for all football clubs and associations. Now it is up to the government to find time to put the proposals into action. ■

SPORTING CHANCE FOR AUSTRALIAN FASHION

The Australian Olympics, 2000, were a triumph for three popular Australian fashion designers. Jenny Kee, Peter Morrisey and Lisa Ho were chosen to represent Australian fashion, by designing outfits for performers in the opening ceremony.

Competition for the job was fierce. The Olympics reach a television audience of up to two billion people around the world. The biggest catwalk shows in Paris wouldn't dream of reaching an audience a tenth of that size. So the lucky winners had something very special for their portfolios.

Then again, they had to work hard to reap the rewards. Even after winning the competition, the three faced a monumental job. The part of the performance they were creating costumes for involved no less than 2,000 performers! ■

The crew of Prada's ITA 45 *yacht put the latest sailing wear to the ultimate test – before it hits the high streets.*

FROM HIGH SEAS TO HIGH STREET

Heavy-duty sportswear and outdoor gear has been gaining a foothold in urban fashions over the last few years. For manufacturers who have to cope with these trends, the big question is, why? Is this some fad, requiring only a temporary increase in their output, or should they be investing heavily to cope with a permanent market?

SPONSORSHIP

What is it about sports gear that appeals to new young consumers? Part of the answer lies in the sponsorship arrangements of sports outfitters such as Nike. Identifying brands with prominent sports personalities was once the province of specialist markets such as golf or tennis enthusiasts. In the mid-1980s, something changed. For starters, black athletes and basketball players began to be paid superstar wages. Sports became a sign of ambition, and young blacks brought sportswear on to the streets and into clubs, where the rest of the market soon took up the style.

But there are further factors influencing the latest growth in the market. Brands such as Helly Hansen have not used big names to attract the money. Their approach is a rigorous attention to clothing technology.

According to John Leaver, their UK MD, 'Our design team works with those at the sharp end – the seafarers, climbers and skiers who actually wear our clothes – to ensure that everything we manufacture meets their demanding criteria.'

EXTREME WEAR

So why are these extreme-weather items selling fast to those of us who think walking to the newsagent's is an exciting adventure? Part of the reason lies in the technology. If you want to dance all night in a club, you're more likely to wear fabrics that are designed for aerobics and other exercise – such as the useful 'wick' effect on some all-weather gear.

But the decisive factor, after all, is that men are finally going shopping for themselves. Research shows that men buy technology. Confused by the range of styles on offer, older men are especially likely to make a decision on the basis of 'features' the clothing offers. The more masculine the features – rugged, survival-orientated – the more comfortable these male consumers feel with their decisions. With the trend for more male shopping firmly established, it looks like sportswear makers can look forward to being very busy in future. ■

WHO'S WHO

The following are some of the organisations concerned with fashion or issues relating to it. The views are varied and we suggest you contact them for more information or visit their websites.

■ **Central St Martin's College of Art and Design**
The college that sets all the trends for young British fashion design, with several very succesful graduates.
Southampton Row, London WC1B 4AP
Enquiries to:
applications@csm.linst.ac.uk
http://www.lcf.linst.ac.uk/cms.cgi/site/

■ **Dazed and Confused**
One look at this magazine's website tells you that this is one of Britain's hottest players in style, aimed at the male market.
111 Old Street, London EC1M 9PH
http://www.confused.co.uk

■ **Delamar Make-Up Academy**
Getting into make-up for fashion or film? You could do worse than a three-month course here with industry experts on hand.
The Make-Up Centre
52a Walham Grove, London SW6 1Q

http://www.themake-upcentre.co.uk

■ **Eating Disorders Association**
A reliable support and information service on any eating disorders.
First Floor, Wensum House, 103 Prince of Wales Road, Norwich NR1 1DW
Youth Helpline 01603 765 050
http//www.edauk.com/

■ **International Apparel Federation**
A trade body linking clothing manufacturers around the world. If you want to mass-produce your designs, you may find your factory here!
5 Portland Place, London W1N 3AA
http://www.iafnet.org/

■ **London College of Fashion**
A close-runner with Central St Martin's for the trophy of best fashion college, the students here are responsible for the excellent N-Touch (see p27).
20 John Princes Street,
London W1M OBJ
http://www.lcf.linst.ac.uk

■ **People for the Ethical Treatment of Animals (PeTA)**
Campaigns protect the rights of all animals, including those killed for their fur. PeTA Europe Ltd, PO Box 3169, London SW18 4WJ
http://www.peta-online.org

Australian fashion is also well represented on the net. Here are some sites to check out.

■ **VOGUE Australia**
Fashion, beauty, features and lifestyle.
www.vogue.com /au

■ **Fashion Australia**
Featuring Australian manufacturers, wholesalers, and agents.
www.ausfashion.com

■ **Miyo**
Global, theme-based magazine that serves the interests of sophisticated, urban modernists and trendsetters.
www.miyomag.com

■ **Netstyle**
Fashion magazine and directory of Australian fashion designers.
www.netstyle.com.au

Note to parents and teachers
Every effort has been made by the Publishers to ensure that these websites are suitable for children; that they are of the highest educational value, and that they contain no inappropriate or offensive material. However, because of the nature of the Internet, it is impossible to guarantee that the contents of these sites will not be altered. We strongly advise that Internet access is supervised by a responsible adult. ■

GO ON, TALK ABOUT IT

The Fashion News doesn't just want to give you its news and views. It wants you, the reader, to talk about them too. Here are some questions to get you going:
■ Do you think fashion encourages the eating disorder anorexia?
■ Is fashion unfair to people with low incomes?
■ Is most fashion directed at women? Why/why not?
■ Is fashion wasteful?
■ What do you think about the use of very young models in fashion?

■ Are 5% of young girls anorexic? How might the statistics get muddled?
■ Do you know if your clothes were manufactured in 'sweatshop' conditions?
■ Have you ever found an aspect of fashion shocking or unacceptable?
■ Do you care what other people think of your appearance? Why?
■ Do you think big can be beautiful?
■ If girls can wear trousers to school, should boys be allowed skirts?
■ Should we use animals in making cosmetics and clothing?

■ Are men's suits boring?
■ Are supermodels paid too much?
■ Would you like a career in fashion?
■ How are famous people affected by fashion and the media?
■ Should usefulness be more or less important than style?
■ Is fashion the same as art?
■ Should fashion be associated with political or charitable causes?
■ Do you go clothes shopping for fun?
■ How pressurised are you to buy the latest thing – whether it is a football strip, a CD or the right length trousers?

WHAT'S WHAT

Here's *The Fashion News'* quick reference aid explaining some terms you'll have come across in its pages.

■ **abolition** The banning or legal ending of a particular practice, such as the slave trade or border controls.

■ **anorexia nervosa** A disease where the fear of weight gain becomes so obsessive that it leads to malnutrition and severe weight loss, first described in 1873. The worst cases can be fatal. Mainly treated by counselling.

■ **breast cancer** A dangerous tumour growing in the breast, most commonly affecting older women, but occasionally found in men. Treatable if diagnosed promptly.

■ **bulimia** Compulsive over-eating, normally accompanied by self-induced vomiting and extreme feelings of guilt. Often linked with anorexia. Treated by counselling.

■ **catwalk** The raised platform or stage along which models parade to show off a new collection.

■ **Chairman Mao** Leader of the Chinese revolution in 1949, who disliked individuality and promoted uniforms for all citizens.

■ **commerce** The buying and selling of goods and services, or business.

■ **compensation** Money paid to an individual or a company to make up for unfair treatment. The money is usually paid by whoever was responsible for the unfair treatment.

■ **consumerism** A system which promotes the ever-increasing buying and consuming of material goods.

■ **creditors** People owed money by a business or individual, often investors.

■ **Dada/Dadaism** An early 20th century art movement based on deliberate foolishness and resistance to logic.

■ **demographic** How a population is made up, for example, the relative sizes of the different age groups or the balance between male and female.

■ **eating disorder** Any health-threatening variance from 'normal' eating behaviour, normally under-eating. See *anorexia nervosa* and *bulimia*.

■ **equal opportunities** Rules designed to stop people being denied fair treatment because of their inherited characteristics, especially gender, race, sexuality and disability.

■ **ethics** Standards of fair practice or good behaviour, similar to morals.

■ **exploitation** Using people unfairly, often those who are not in a position to fight back, in order to make yourself richer.

■ **haute couture** From the French words 'high' and 'sewing', the highest and most expensive form of fashion, designer-led and usually made to measure (i.e. to fit a specific individual).

■ **Human rights** The freedoms and legal protection we believe all human beings deserve, whatever the local political system.

■ **Inland Revenue** The government department which collects taxes from every taxpayer.

■ **Islamic veil** A headscarf worn by many Muslim women for modesty, around or across the face.

■ **liposuction** A medical procedure, usually used for cosmetic reasons, in which fat is sucked out of the body by a kind of vacuum cleaner.

■ **merchandise** Goods bought and sold. Now most commonly used in the form 'merchandising', where a popular character or organisation (such as a football team) is used to brand objects for sale, such as shirts.

■ **milliner** A hat designer or hat maker.

■ **modernist** Art and design which breaks from the past, often using very simple themes.

■ **NSPCC** The National Society for the Prevention of Cruelty to Children, a charity working to protect children from harm and abuse.

■ **paparazzi** The name given to the group of photographers, often self-employed, who take and sell photos of celebrities to newspapers.

■ **peers** Your friends and people in a similar group to you, for example in the same age group.

■ **psychotherapist** A counsellor who aims to help emotional disorders by any of a range of methods, including one-to-one discussion or leading group therapy.

■ **rag trade** The clothing industry.

■ **retail** The sale of goods to a consumer (i.e. the last person to buy something). Retail is often used to refer to outlets where consumers buy things, for example shops.

■ **self-employed** Working for yourself either in your own small business or freelance for other people, where you pay your tax and national insurance, not your employer.

■ **subcontract** Passing elements of a project to another supplier. For example, when a clothing manufacturer cannot produce the goods needed fast enough it may subcontract to another supplier.

■ **subsidiary** A small company within a larger business with its own brand or identity.

■ **sweatshop** Small, labour-intensive factory, particularly common in clothing and leather-work industries.

■ **union** An organisation formed by employees to give them more bargaining power with employers. Some larger unions operate beyond a single company and support a particular trade or profession on a national basis.

■ **webcam** A simple digital video camera which can be connected to give low-quality transmission over the internet.

INDEX